Hymns

of

SAINT EPHREM THE SYRIAN

translated by

MARY HANSBURY

SLG Press
Convent of the Incarnation
Fairacres Parker Street
Oxford OX4 1TB England
www.slgpress.co.uk

ISBN 978-0-7283-0167-2
ISSN 0307-1405

The icon on the front cover was written by Mary Hansbury, using a traditional sixteenth-century motif to depict an early manuscript which describes Saint Ephrem's gift to us, saying that a vine went up from him and 'every creature under heaven was sated by it It bore abundant clusters and even the birds of the sky came and ate of its fruit. The more they ate the more its clusters increased.'

Introduction

Praise and thanksgiving play a central role in the traditions of the religions of the world throughout the ages. The Christian saint, Teresa of Avila writes often of praise. In the *Interior Castle* she says: 'The soul would desire to have a thousand lives so as to employ them all for God, and that everything here on earth would be a tongue to help it praise Him.'[1]

No less significant a voice of thanksgiving can be found in the Jewish tradition. Abraham Isaac Kook, a renowned twentieth-century Rabbi, commenting on a portion of the Talmud says: 'Other peoples eat in order to satisfy their craving for food; the blessing or "grace", after the meal, is an afterthought. Jews eat in order to be able to bless God.'[2]

St Ephrem (306-373), an outstanding religious poet of the Syriac Church was born in Nisibis and spent most of his life there ministering as a deacon until his death in Edessa. In these hymns, attributable to him, we even find a singular interpretation of the fall of Adam: his sin was that 'he ate fruit and did not give praise'. The ingratitude of Adam was redeemed by Christ when He 'gave praise and broke bread'.[3] Both of these moments are brought together in the Commentary on the Diatessaron:

> It was because Adam had not blessed the fruit at the time
> when, as a rebel, he gathered it, that our Lord blessed the
> bread and broke it. The bread entered into them making up
> for the avarice by which Adam had rejected God.[4]

According to Ephrem, to praise God is the role of humanity, angels, seraphim and the natural world.[5] For human beings who have free will, not to praise God is a choice for death:

> While I live I will give praise,
>   and not be as if I had no existence;
> I will give praise during my lifetime,
>   and will not be
> a dead man among the living.[6]

Yet, Ephrem is ever mindful that right praise is a gift from God to be invoked. And in the face of human inadequacy, in one of his hymns he asks Christ to fill our mouths with praise as He filled the jars with wine at Cana:

I have invited You, Lord,
>   to a wedding-feast of song,
> but the wine — the utterance of praise —
>   at our feast has failed.
> You are the guest
>   who filled the jars with good wine
> Fill my mouth with Your praise.[7]

Even the freedom to praise, once it has been bestowed, is linked to the gift of Baptism when the 'robe of glory' is regained which Isaiah calls the 'mantle of praise'.[8] Ephrem seeks continually to see Christ through Scripture and nature, and to give Him praise and thanksgiving.[9]

Background

Here are eleven hymns of thanksgiving which come to us from the fourth century. They describe a type of liturgical or Christian practice — an *agape* — rather than the Eucharist, but more than a simple meal of Christians. Authorship of these hymns has been variously ascribed. But the work of Pierre Yousif seems to give them a secure place among the writings of St Ephrem. He has identified numerous themes which are traceable to Ephrem and his school, and Yousif maintains that at least Hymns 3-11 cannot seriously be questioned.[10]

Most notably in Ephrem's Hymn on the Church, there is a description of Christian hospitality in the image of Christ in the Eucharist, resulting in an *agape*-type situation not unlike those in these Table Blessings. As noted by Yousif, already the third-century Syriac Didascalia speaks of an *agape*. In subsequent centuries, an *agape* can be found in Syriac tradition at least until the twelfth century.[11] Finally there is the witness of St Ignatius of Antioch. In his letter to the Church at Smyrna, he speaks of an *agape* and includes it in the same context as Baptism, which may indicate the importance of the *agape* in the Christian community at that time.

Yousif concludes his article by exhorting contemporary seminaries, monasteries, parishes and homes to revive this liturgical practice. And one might add, on a quiet day of prayer anyone might pray these blessings alone over a meal, renewing a deeper personal sense of gratitude and praise, so absent from our various cultures.

Many of the themes which appear in these Table Blessings can be found throughout the works of Ephrem. Numerous citations are made in the Notes. Here are mentioned a few central ideas which are implicit all through the Blessings. Others have noted how this iconic symbolic thought seems to be particularly suited to our times. Ephrem approaches the mystery of God by praise and wonder rather than investigation. There is an ontological gap or chasm between God and creatures. By this, Ephrem indicates the fundamental difference between Creator and created, as stated in Luke 16: 26.[12] But Jesus becomes the bridge over the chasm, and God's descent into our language at the Incarnation enables us to speak of Him. Especially, He puts on names that we may put on His names. So there is an exchange of names but the name of Jesus itself becomes the bridge:

> O Jesus, the glorious name!
> The hidden bridge which causes to pass over
> from death to life.[13]

Those familiar with the invocation of the Name may not know of Ephrem as an early link in the tradition, preparing this way of calling on the Name.[14]

Yet God my king is from of old working salvation in the midst of the earth. (Ps. 74: 12)

According to Ephrem, God 'puts on names' in the Old Testament, and is described in metaphorical language consistent with human experience, by way of condescension to the limits of human understanding. In the Incarnation, God goes on to clothe Himself in the human body. Finally, as a result of the Incarnation, God makes Himself available to humanity in the Mysteries (*râzê*) of Baptism and Eucharist. And these Mysteries remain present and active within humanity and the natural world.[15]

In addition, all the types (*tupsê*) throughout Scripture, and the symbols (*râzê*) in creation are gathered in Christ. Once incarnated in Him, they become present and active in all humanity and creation, through the Sacraments (*râzê*). This is a major theme in Ephrem's teaching. See for example his Hymn on Virginity 28. 2:

The scattered mysteries (*rāzê*) from the Torah,
You have gathered beside Your beauty;
The figures (*tapn<u>k</u>ê*) which are in Your
Gospel You have put forth. And forces (*haïlê*)
And signs (*rušmê*) from nature, You have mixed
like pigments for Your image (*surtâ*).[16]

With types and symbols, both Scripture and nature are set forth here, all converging at the Incarnation, then to be released within humanity and the world, through the Sacraments within the Church.[17] These eleven hymns clearly do not describe the Eucharist, but they do concern a liturgical situation carrying many features of Ephrem's deeply Christological view of reality and how it is transmitted, becoming the locus of potential divinization for all.[18]

Behold my covenant is with you, and you shall be the father of many nations. (Gen.17: 4)

At Abraham's becoming head, by God's blessing, of the people of Israel, God made him father of many nations. God chose one people for his own, but all its privileges were destined to be extended to all the nations. According to Ephrem's exegesis, and that of Aphrahat before him, God's plan for the salvation of the world was to choose and to train one nation in order to bring his grace to all.[19] And God's choice of Israel is not seen as complete in itself, nor is it suppressed, but it is accomplished in Christ and continued in the Sacraments.[20]

Early Syriac Christianity in Nisibis, where Ephrem spent more than fifty years, was Jewish in character because of its proximity to the Jewish community there. In the past it has been argued that Ephrem's description of Jews and Judaism, as evidenced in *Memre* VII and VIII of this collection, are based on personal experience, that Judaism posed a threat to the local Christian community and that there was even Jewish proselytism among Christians. Recent scholarship now tends to see Ephrem's language towards Jews, which can be bitter and unjust, as more in terms of intra-Christian struggle between Nicene and Arian Christians, and that he uses negative language about biblical Jews to denounce, in reality, the Arians who are posing a threat to his Nicene Christianity.[21]

Although certain of Ephrem's polemics may have developed in relation to the socio-political-ecclesial context in fourth-century Nisibis, early Christianity did see itself as the 'theological opposite of Judaism giving rise to a polar structure which was anti-Judaistic'.[22] And, differing from the Greek tradition of setting boundaries and defining God, Ephrem used his poetic skills of symbolism and paradox in order to make the characteristics of the Church stand out in this 'typology of opposition'.[23] In his study of Jacob of Serug, who often explicates some of the earlier theology of St Ephrem, T. Bou Mansour notes the same bitter and unjust language of Jacob towards the Jews: Jacob's unrelenting criticism of the Jews for their literal interpretation of Scripture and their not understanding its typology. Ephrem, like Jacob, seems to share a hesitation about whether Jews were ever cut off. But Bou Mansour concludes by noting the homily of Jacob of Serug concerning Leah and Rachel which features Jacob marrying the two sisters, showing that the Son will take the People and the Peoples, which Jacob calls a 'great mystery' (*râzâ*):[24]

> Here a type of the two assemblies
> was accomplished, in the two sisters
> which were given to one man.
>
> A great mystery shone in the two sisters
>   who were taken.
> That deed was the shadow of a great body;
>   except it be so, it could not have come to pass.
>
> For that beautiful thing which was done
>   was not Jacob's doing,
> The mystery entered with the righteous man
>   into the pagan's house,
> and it betrothed the two maidens
>   that it might evidently show itself.
>
> The Nation and the nations were signified
>   by Leah and Rachel;
> the Synagogue and the Church were heralded
>   in the two sisters.[25]

The translation of these *Memre* was made from the Syriac text as found in *L'Orient Syrien*, where Latin and French translations are included: L. Mariès, L. Froman, F. Graffin, 'Mimré de saint Éphrem sur la bénédiction de la table', *L'Orient_Syrien* 4 (1959): pp.73-109; 163-192; 285-295.

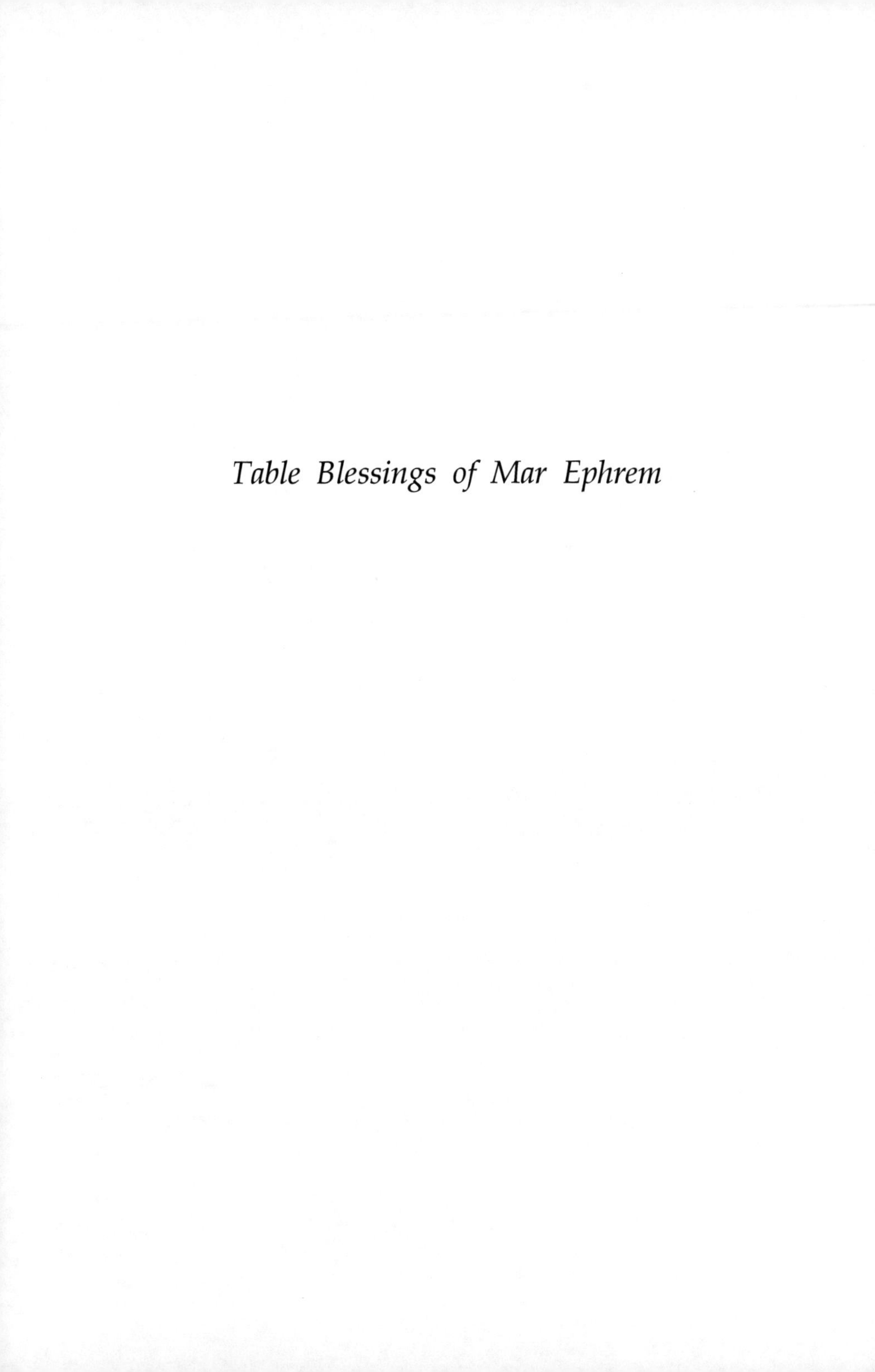

Table Blessings of Mar Ephrem

Memra I

Blessed is the Good One
Who has stretched out His hands
and made our table so very glorious.

1.

All who are filled by His gift,
give glory to His Essence.[1]
And all who have eaten of His good things,
let them give thanks for His grace.
Whoever has drunk of His spring,
may that spring of His words overflow to him.[2]
And all who are filled at His table,
let them praise Him with His psalms.
Let the one before whom delights are heaped,
distribute some of them as blessings;
and the one whose table is full,
let him give alms from it.
Who loves the fruit of the vine,
let him love hymns of thanksgiving;
and whoever drinks abundantly,
let him love to give praise in abundance.
Who loves to pick up again the cup,
let him love to pick up again the Law.
May the whole host of food lovers
utter sounds of praise!

2.

While drinking chaste wine,
spiritual hymns are appropriate.
Let us not eat like animals
who eat and drink without giving praise.
An animal, when it has taken its fill, keeps silent;
rather let our mouth give thanks that we have been filled.[3]
Let us not be similar to the evil serpent
who ate without giving thanks;

nor to the bird who ate
and yet refused to give praise.
On the banquet table,
let us spread the story of His benefits.
Let us not just nourish the body;
let the soul also feed on teachings.
As the cup gladdens the mouth,
let exegesis delight the ear.
Let all who recline at our table,
extend their words as well as their hands;
and as they are eager for food,
let them also be eager for interpretation of Scripture.

3.

Let the one who presides at the feast
be the cause of the benefits.
Let propriety start off from the very beginning
lest boldness settle in.
Let justice open its door,
but let impudence be ashamed.
Let the first begin first,
and then each one according to his capacity.
Let peace minister in their midst
to extinguish contention there.
Let love reign at the feast!
Let truth admonish the listeners
lest there be any favouritism.[4]

4.

Whoever is a child, let him be quiet
and by listening acquire life;
let him be a listener,
and keep silence at the feast.
Let the one who is sad not sow
sloth among his companions;
and let the idle talker not disturb
the sweetness of the feast.

Whoever is learned in the Scriptures,
let him fill the office of expositor;
and whoever is rich in resources,
let him be mindful of the one who is untaught;
whose mind is sound,
let it be to him a crucible for testing.

5.

The one whose judgement is steadfast,
let him still the disturbance of arguers;
and the one who needs to question,
let him open the speaker's treasure.
Neither lengthy questions
nor obscure explanations;
let the question be brief and clear,
the explanation sweet sounding and correct.
Let disputation seek beryls
and discovery, pearls.
Let interpretation be a fountain,
and may it irrigate thirsty ears.
Let the debate cast its brightness,
illumining the eyes of the mind.

6.

Let one speak about sobriety,
and another about purity.
At our table let there be spoken of
that table of the Kingdom.[5]
And at that feast let them remember
the rich man and Lazarus.[6]
Let them call to mind that one who had said:
'I was hungry and you gave me to eat.'[7]
Let sobriety come in and cast out
gluttony from among them.
At this feast let them
call to mind the great feast of Abraham.[8]

7.

   May intemperance not come in:
   it would weary those at the feast.
   Let wine not come in
   to debase those who are honourable.
   When they drink, let them also
   call to mind Jonadab[9] and his commands:
   that Jeremiah was the cupbearer
   and prepared cups and vessels,
   but the true sons of Jonadab
   kept wine from their mouths.
   Since they have not tasted it at all,
   may we drink it in moderation.

8.

   Let us refuse an excess of it,
   since they rejected it completely.
   Also the Nazirites are remembered,[10]
   who completely rejected the vine.
   But its use did not defile,
   since there is a great mystery in its clusters.
   The Apostle bade his disciple
   to drink a modest amount.[11]
   Remember the corruption
   which wine brought upon Noah and Lot.[12]
   Of these things, and such as these,
   let there be spoken at our table.

9.

   Thus there will be help for those who listen,
   and profit for those who preach;
   for all the company, a banquet,
   spiritual as well as corporal;
   for the invited, gain,
   for those of the household, blessings;
   a good vintage for one's friends,
   for the heavenly Watchers,[13] praise,

and bequests for mankind;
to God thanksgiving,
and praise to His Christ.
Even for me, let there be in prayer
a remembrance at your feasts.

Memra II

1.

Blessed is the One who has filled our feast
with sustenance from His treasury!
Guests, prepare your ears
and your mouths to sing praise.
Be receivers and givers;
render glory for what He has provided.

2.

God gave from His treasure;
give, also you, from your treasures.
For God, deeds are simple;
and, for you, a hymn of thanksgiving.
God gave as He wished;
give, also you, as you are able.

3.

Since He has done hard things for us,
instead of created things which are difficult for us,
give thanks which is easy.
He exacts not in the measure that He has lent.

4.

Give praise for His provisions,
which He gave you according to His pleasure.
Indeed you have been filled,
give thanks with a hymn.
The vine and the wheat for His part,
prayer and love for our part.
The seed and the olive from His treasure,
the sound of praise from our treasure.
His command yields a tasty meal,
let our will give praise.
Rain and dew from His heaven,
let thanksgiving go up from us.
Pleasures from His will
and shouts of joy from our free will!

5.

The guests are grateful
to the one who gives food for one day.
To the one who gives ordinary water,
no one refuses a thank you.
Who then would refuse a gift
to the Donor who sustains the universe?[1]
To the one who gives a cup of water,
God promises a reward.[2]
Who would refuse to thank God
whose gift is greater than all?
The gift which we give Him,
though contemptible, He does not disdain it.
Who would diminish his thanks
to the One who gives abundantly?

6.

To one who gives us something,
we thank him with a full mouth.
Let us fill our mouth with praise
for the One who has proffered[3] us everything.
What profit to the one who eats,
if he eats and withholds a thank offering?
May our praise not be impoverished,
lest our table be depleted.
Let us give thanks to the One in want of nothing,
that He may fill our deficiency.
If we refuse Him, He is not diminished;
but if He withholds, who can survive?
Let us give thanks for our food,
and for our drink, praise.

7.

For our gathering, our supplication;
and our psalmody to the One who summons us!
Blessed be He who has filled our feast
with supplies from His sustenance!
Glory to Him from our table,
to the Father, to the Son and to the Holy Spirit!

Memra III

1.

Behold, my brothers, the body and the soul,
the table, but also the instruction.
The table for the visible body,
for the hidden heart, instruction.[1]
To those whom our Lord made recline,
let our company be similar, my beloved.
They were astonished and satiated:[2]
they had been nourished in body as well as in soul.
For in that bread which multiplied
a great marvel was hidden.
The body was satisfied by visible things,
and the soul was pleased by hidden things.
The body did not stop from eating,
nor the mind from marvelling.

2.

The mouth did not stop taking food,
nor the tongue giving praise.
If had been weighed there
thanksgiving together with the food,
O my brothers, the praise
would have far surpassed the food.
For not according as they ate
did they thus only give praise:
they gave praise a hundredfold!
When they saw the bread, they snatched and ate it;
they were speechless and marvelled when they saw the sign.
Let this our banquet, my beloved, resemble theirs.

3.

Truly let us marvel, and give thanks,
that fullness flows from any stalk;
that wine springs from a vine-shoot,
and all our delights from a piece of wood.[3]

Truly this is a great miracle,
as the miracle which our Lord performed.
For then He was working openly
yet every day He does it in secret.
With that wine in the jars,
He increased praise in the drinkers.[4]
A little wine in the jars,
and great praise in the drinkers!
The jars become vines
for our Lord who performs new things.

4.

Blessed be the vine-dresser[5] who in the same day
planted a vineyard and pressed out the wine.
Thus it is right for the one who eats
to eat, to marvel and to praise.
Likewise it is fitting for the drinker
to drink, to marvel and to bless
the miracle of fatness from a dry stalk,
and the fermenting of wine from a piece of wood;
the moist from the dry,
and the unctuous from the shrivelled.
Beasts are too blind of understanding
to receive food through a miracle.
For an animal is too deprived of intelligence
to be aware of these seeds.
The one who eats while dazed
resembles a bewildered animal.
And the one who drinks indiscreetly,
his drinking is like that of a beast.
Do you eat like an animal?
Then eat raw meat.
And if you are like a beast,
then eat also its food.

5.

But if your food is different,
let your thanksgiving be never-ending!
And if you have drunk with discernment,
give praise again as if with understanding.
Your food is different from that of beasts,
yet your mouth is silent like theirs.
You have not drunk like the animals
but like them you are mute.
Not only in food and drink
are you better than the animals,
but in love and praise,
and in hymns and psalms.
Man seeks what is of the body,
though he is greater than (wild) animals.
But if the body seeks what is its own,
let the mind seek its own.
The body does not neglect its place,
lest it suffer dishonour with the animals;
it seeks indeed its own honour
for it does not behave like them.
Ought the mind to diminish itself,
even becoming like dogs?

6.

It is more than enough that our father Adam
became like the animals;[6]
since he ate fruit[7] but did not give praise,
may you give praise for everything.
Indeed he did not praise God,
for as a rebel he had eaten
more ungratefully than the animals
who are obedient to their masters.
Since Adam gathered but did not praise,
our Saviour gave praise[8] and broke bread.[9]
As He had made restitution for his debts,
so over the bread He bestowed thanksgiving.

Instead of the one who refuses to give praise,
who will dedicate praise?
For all of us was rendered
this praise which our Lord sang.
If we have not given thanks at our table,
His table does not welcome us.
But if we give thanks at our table,
the Good One will make us worthy of His table.
Since we praised Him for our enjoyment,
He, the Living One, will make us worthy of His delight.
Praise be to Him here and hereafter,
thanksgiving in both worlds!

Memra IV

1.

Turn, my brothers, towards praise,
you who have returned to food.
Since our heart is with the bread,
let it also be with thanksgiving.
And as drinking is pleasant and sweet,
may praising thus be cherished.
And as gemstones are delightful,
even more so are psalms.
Hymns more than sweet savours,
thanksgiving more than sweet meats!
And rather than bread which is more pleasing than all,
may that love which gives life to all be desired.

2.

No one has eaten slackly,
let no one give praise drowsily.
Because we have eaten vigorously, my brothers,
let us give praise attentively.
Gone is the hunger which was upsetting,
let our thanksgiving not be disturbed.
And the troubling thirst has abated,
let our praise not be hindered.

Indeed before bread it was right
that our mouth radiantly give thanks,
how much more now that we are satisfied
should we radiantly give praise!

3.

The just ones blessed when they were hungry;
let us give thanks when we are filled.
For them, water and dry vegetables;[1]
but for us, tasty treats and juices.
Instead of the barley cake of Elijah[2],
blessed is the One who has multiplied delights for us!
And instead of the food of the son of Buzi,[3]
blessed is the One who has increased pleasures for us!
There was great hunger in Samaria,[4]
blessed is the One who has satisfied our dwelling!
And like the horn and the pitcher which overflowed,[5]
blessed is the One who has poured good things on us!
Instead of soup in a pot
and flour in a cloth,[6]
blessed is he who has arranged
all kinds of good things in our dishes.

4.

Instead of Herod's platter
which brought death to the guests,[7]
blessed is He who brought to our banquet
utensils full of delights.
Instead of the insatiability of the sons of Eli,
who had snatched the raw meat,[8]
blessed is He who discreetly gives us meat,
which is modest and prepared with care!
Instead of the People[9] who were nauseous and vomited,[10]
behold the moderation at our table.
And while they ate, drank and diverted themselves,[11]
let us eat, drink and give praise.
Instead of cymbals before the calf,[12]

let our harp chant for our Lord.
And instead of greedy songs,
let praise resound from our assembly.

Memra V

1.

Behold a miracle in the bread, my brothers,
and within the drink a marvel:
the taste of bread and wine,
the mouth has perceived clearly;
the creation of the bread and wine,
let the heart regard secretly with wonder.
In everything which comes prepared for us,
let us see two matters in it:
let us eat the bread and give praise,
for it comes out of the lowly soil;
let us drink the wine and bless,
for it comes forth from the paps (juice) of the vine.

2.

Let us also give praise for oil,
which flows from the rugged thorn bush.
Let us give thanks to Him for everything
which is prepared with fire.[1]
For while fire is not edible,
it gives taste to the cooked food.
The heat is in the taste
while the fire is not extinguished.
It is there and not there,
this fire within the cooked food.
Its heat is close at hand
but its flame is far away.
Its power dwells hidden there
while depicting a revealed mystery.
Heat is similar in strength to fire,
but in nothing else is it like it.
In heat and power it is similar
but in colour, not at all.
Because of these things
let the one who eats marvel,

let the one who drinks be amazed by them.
Let us eat, drink and praise
the Lord of these things and those!

3.

It is the Evil One, my brothers, who teaches us
to harm ourselves by food.
For where one ought to be declared righteous,
there he leads us into sin;
And where it is right to bless,
there he teaches curses.
Insipid, with or without salt,
everyone there is to be reviled!
On the inner things and the outer ones,
accusation or reproofs!
For our wine and for our table,
it was right we should remember the Father!

4.

When someone eats or drinks,
he does not taste the flesh of animals.
Saul, with the meat which he ate,[2]
had eaten the flesh of David;[3]
and with the wine which he drank openly,
he was drinking his blood secretly.
When the brothers of Joseph sat down to eat,[4]
they secretly ate his flesh;
they sold him, and sat and relaxed,
and were delighted that they had rejected him.[5]

5.

Since the day when they heard his dreams,
only in this day, was bread pleasing to them.
He did not requite them their wrongdoings
as they refreshed themselves at his table.
The bread of Egypt did not please him
as did what he ate with his brothers.
And the wine of Pharaoh did not please him

as did what he drank with his beloved ones.
Fairer to him was the crown of his brothers
than the diadem on Pharaoh's head.

6.

In the drink which he sipped with his brothers,
he had mixed love for them with the wine.
The wine which he drank was not as sweet to him
as his delight when he saw them.
For the wine he enjoyed a little,
but love for them, very much more.
The one who drinks sees his beloved:
with the wine he drinks love.
But if he sees his enemies,
he sips anger with his drink.

7.

Let us mix the wine in our cups
with the fair love for our beloved ones.
Let the wine run in our veins,[6]
but love flow in our thoughts.
Let the food go to the belly,
but let prayer remain in the mind.
If our food is tasteless,
may there be relish in our mind.
If we contend with the insipid
also our thinking is insipid.
And if we are angry with those who are seasoned,
our mind is neither seasoned nor discerning.
And if we find fault with those who are hollow,
this is not a food of eternity.
Because what belongs to eternity is hidden
it seems insipid even tasteless;
while the sensations of this life seem seasoned
though they are only for a day.
How long of these things
and such as these will we speak, my brothers?

Enough of this rebuke,
for I speak but do not act!

Memra VI

1.

My brothers, since we began with integrity,
then let us conclude discreetly.
Since before our bread we gave a blessing,
let us give thanks after having eaten.
Between thanksgiving and praise,
let us place our food in the middle.
Between praise and shouts of joy,
let us modestly take our beverage.
At the very beginning, praise,
and at the end, thanksgiving!

2.

The People[7] began backwards
and likewise concluded badly.
For before they ate they did not give praise,
and after they were filled they did not bless.
The meat which they ate did them no good[8]
because they did not bless its Giver.
He gave drink from the Rock,[9]
but they drank without wonder or thanksgiving.
Let us give thanks to Him for his founts,
for their treasures never end.

3.

Not because He has need of blessings,
But He wanted to teach us what is right.
For how is one diminished
who with his food gives thanks?
Not at a great price does he buy
this praise which is gratis.
The door of the Merciful One is open,[10]
who by our thanksgiving exalts us.
For as He gives us food,
He also increases our chanting of praise;
And as the bread openly gives life

so praise gives us life in secret.
He who scorns praise
therefore scorns bread!

4.

The bread testifies concerning praise,[11]
that souls live by it.
Without bread the body is dead,
without praise the soul is ill.
The gluttonous one is concerned with the body
and one who fasts, with the soul.
Meat makes the glutton grow strong
but doctrine strengthens the wise one.
For the glutton, chewed food and blood,
for the pure one, praise and thanksgiving.
Food and thanksgiving
let us give to the soul and to the body.
With food and prayer
the body and the mind flourish.

5.

The body is nourished with toil,
the spirit and the soul without toil.
Without sowing or without reaping,
the wind[12] gives life to souls.
So that from time to time there are fruits,
but prayers at all times.
Weighty matters are light
and what is easy is hard for us.
With great efforts, food,
without effort, thanksgiving!
To Him praise from the sluggish
who are quick to the table!
Give praise, lazy ones,
since you have eaten so well.

1.

The ungrateful ones saw the cluster[1] of grapes:
that sight of which astonishes all.
But they did not bless its Maker,
nor did they praise its artisan;
they praised the molten calf
and its builder they blessed.[2]
Yet the cluster of grapes was thick,
beauty together with abundance.

2.

As beautiful as is the pearl,
its beauty is not edible;
but the beauty of a grape[3]
is a fount of all good things.
A beryl is fair to look at
though its beauty is without taste;
in the vine's treasures are hidden,
torrents of every delight.
The tabernacle was decorated by Him
with inedible gems;
but to the People He brought fruits,
edible and delicious.
He chose for Himself what was inedible
to show that He hungered not;
but to man He gave all,
to show that he is in need of all.

3.

The harmonious cluster of grapes rebuked
the People[4] whose mind is divided.
All the grapes thus united
had entered the divided assembly.
The cluster was beautiful and orderly;
the People were agitated and disorderly.
In the cluster, sweetness;
in the People, bitterness.[5]

4.

At the sight yet again of the cluster,
the People were even more perturbed.
At these silent and serene fruits,
the People clamoured all the more.
They neglected the praise which was due,
and the song of praise which was fitting.
Instead of praise, they complained;
instead of thanksgiving, they murmured.

5.

The vine which went forth from Eygpt,[6]
its grapes are bitter grapes.
The cluster with its poles, manifested
the mystery of the beautiful Cross.
It showed itself to the fig trees and they sighed,
whereas they ought to have exulted.
They saw the fig trees in the foul desert
but, ungrateful, they were not comforted.
As the grapes, namely those in the desert,
so also the first-fruits of the figs!
God longed for their face;
but they, for the face of the calf.
They saw the fruits but they did not bless;
though hungry, they did not give praise.
How did the tender plant shoot up,
or how did it gather its sweetness?
Who dyes the colours
of stones without pigments?
And who generates sweetness
from tough roots;
or from fibres, still bitter,
who makes a sweet drink flow?

6.

But therein the True One has mingled
the truth which they never kept.
The sons of Jacob, of Isaac and of Abraham

had changed the truth into falsehood.
Their roots were sweet,
but their fruits bitter.
The root of Abraham was fair,
and the branches of Sarah, sweet.
But bitter was the outcry
of this People, offspring of Abraham;
passionate was their murmuring
against Moses who was from Sarah.
The People saw the cluster
but did not earnestly desire it;
they were yearning for garlic and onions.
The People saw the fig trees but did not desire them,
they were eager for leeks;
what was a gift from God,
though excellent, they were not pleased with.
They had yearned for garlic and onions,
to eat in the midst of the Gentiles.
Because their soul was dried up they were murmuring,
and seeing the fruits, they were embittered.

7.

Which now of the two
will be accepted, O ungrateful one?[7]
If your soul is dried up, accept
the abundant rich fruits.
But if you hate fruits,
it's because your soul is full of hateful things.
Figs and grapes if elsewhere disliked,
in the desert are much enjoyed.
How very beautiful these things,
precious in their nature!
Sweet fruits did not make sweet
their bitter wills;
the fig tree gave sweetness
but their mind, bitterness.
With good figs He rebuked
the wicked who acted ungratefully.

Memra VIII

1.

Render, my brothers, a song of praise
for the makings of a meal which have entered before us.
Let us not be like the Hebrews
who murmured against the desirable bread.
To the circumcised He had given the manna,
but they did not marvel at its preparation.
It is one, with many flavours,
but they were not amazed at its distinctions.
It served as both bread and as cooked food,
but they did not acknowledge its varieties.
Its colour revealed each condiment,
but they did not give praise for its blending.
There was grumbling instead of wonder,
and instead of praise, murmuring.

2.

The serpents bit them,[1]
but the serpents had not murmured about the dust.
Again, that fire consumed them[2]
which makes everything delicious.
Yet again, the earth devoured them[3]
which was silent while being trampled on by them.
They had fallen in that formidable desert
which, though desolate, was not murmuring.
They were tormented by the quails which they requested;
the food distressed those who ate it.[4]
Men of flesh, they asked for flesh,
and they ate it like a wild animal.
But since they had not marvelled when they ate it,
it was going out from their nostrils.[5]

3.

Because their mouth did not give praise,
the food was bitter to the palate.
The nose which is above the mouth,

condemns the mouth for not giving praise.
Contrary to nature it vomited
the flesh which it had eaten naturally.
What He had given in an unaccustomed way,
the greedy ones wickedly gathered.
They did not praise the Master of the natures,
who changed there the order of nature.
He gave us a type[6] in the elements,
that we might give praise about our food.
Before the bread and after the bread,
He indicated to give praise.

4.

For much and for little,
it was right to give praise;
the greedy one for his fullness,
but the wise one for his hunger.
That rich one did not bless
for his table, on account of his greed.[7]
But Lazarus, that one at his gate,
was yearning for morsels.
And though he did not receive the scraps,
he offered praise instead of resentment.
While the people murmured from their fullness,
Lazarus in his hunger blessed.
We who are filled, let us give praise
as that one did even without scraps.
How much should we give thanks, we who also have much,
let us give especial praise!
If we murmur about our table,
by Lazarus He will judge us.
For he had hunger and pain,
trials and poverty;
and we, feasting and honour,
a heaping up and good health.

5.

Blessed is the One who has given us so much,
and to whom we have given so little.
The measure of our praise is our mouth,
and the dimension of our word is our tongue;
we have extended it boldly
that it might reach the unreachable!
The search though hard is easy,
prayer is hard though easy.
Our wonder, which is helpful, is small
while continual searching is plentiful;
it has wearied love and love has fled,
then pride entered and built a nest in us.
Concord flew away
and contention unfolded its wings.
Scrutiny[8] befell us — and we remained with it,
so did hateful controversy — and it held us back.
For its measure a day does not suffice,
at the expense of what is sweet and pleasant.
Blessed is the one who seeks what is easy!
Blessed is the one who desires what is plain!
For thanksgiving is the measure of our strength,
may our mouth give praise!

Memra IX

1.

For the silent fruits, let us give
praise to the One who adorns the universe.
Let the subject of Paradise be expounded,
concerning the fruits and their beauties;
and about the kinds of fruits and their fragrances
also about the fruits and their flavours.
Speak on account of this (earthly) paradise,
about the true Paradise!
And speak in the temporal garden,
on account of the trees expound:
about the tree of knowledge,
and about the fact that Adam ate it.
(The tree of knowledge) has cast toil upon the labourer.
Render thanksgiving in Paradise!
For the fig trees give praise,
in your brother's stead give praise,
since Adam was silent in the midst of the fig trees,
because of the leaves with which he was clothed give praise.
For the ungrateful ones while silent,
are empty of praise;
but in the discerning one who sings praise,
all creation is a harp.
Creation gives praise to its Maker
with sounds full of wonder.

Memra X

1.

O Good One, who in Your mercy sustain
beings: above and those below,[1]
and distribute the treasure of Your mercy
to men and animals:
bless the table of Your servants
from which Your worshippers have taken delight!
In the dwelling where Your disciples have entered,
make peace and welfare.
Increase Your bounty at their feast
because, my Lord, it refreshes the sons of Your Church.

2.

Receive, my Lord, their offerings
like Abel the just one.[2]
And increase, my Lord, their tithes
in the manner of righteous Job.[3]
May those who eat be satisfied
as were the multitudes in the midst of the desert![4]
May the one who has an abundance increase and be
blessed,
like the morsels which were gathered.
As you blessed the jar and the cruse[5]
by means of Elijah the prophet,

3.

and neither the jar of meal came to an end
nor did the cruse of oil diminish,
until the Lord gave rain
and dew over all the earth:[6]
bless the harvest of Your servants
which Your worshippers have enjoyed!
With the blessings with which Moses blessed
the twelve tribes of Jacob,[7]
may this dwelling be blessed
which has honoured, my Lord, the sons of Your Church.

4.

And as Moses pardoned Reuben[8]
who died at the time of Jacob,
pardon, our Lord, their dead
and have mercy upon their living ones.
May they rejoice with You in Your bridal chamber[9]
on that day when Your brightness will reign.
May they return then to the grace
of the Son of the Living God;
for no one can comprehend
the great sea of Your mercy.

5.

O One, who as man was invited
to the wedding feast with His disciples,
and there worked a sign
as God, the Creator!
O Celestial One, who came
and filled the need at the wedding feast;[10]
who from water did make wine,
and gladdened all the marriage feast:
wonder seized the guests
for the new sign which was done!

6.

When He taught the multitudes in the desert,
He worked amazing miracles:
twice He had filled
the multitudes with a little bread.
And no one can exhaust
that bread which He had multiplied.
When they carried it, not even the Apostles
perceived how they were made to abound.
This is hidden from men.[11]
They received the morsels from our Lord,
as the reading attests to us.[12]

7.

Thus it is, in truth,
for the one who has understanding:
from the hands of the Apostles
the bread has increased and abounded;
from their hands they were casting it
to these crowds who were reclining on the ground.

8.

And when He was invited to the house of Zacchaeus,
He showed there a sign:
there He changed the plunderers
and made them givers;
Zacchaeus gave back the fourfold
of all which he possessed.[13]

9.

And about him our Saviour spoke
in the upper room[14] before his disciples:
the whole reason why God sent
his Only-Begotten to clothe a body,[15]
was to turn everyone from his iniquity[16],
and to restore what was lost.[17]

Memra XI

1.

Come let us hear what our Lord said in His Gospel:
'Who receives a righteous one
in the name of the Righteous One — I say —
will receive the reward of a righteous one
in the great day of the resurrection.'[18]
Great was the charity of those of former times
who welcomed others with simplicity.
For Abraham did not question,
but angels and men
welcomed in like manner.[19]
Nor did righteous Job
bring this to mind,
but all who were coming
he would receive with joy.

2.

The farmers were wise
who trusting, buried their seed:
for when His Kingdom will be revealed,
the seed will result in a hundredfold.[20]
They will reap joys there
that do not pass away, nor are dissolved.
The one who brings offerings,
let him approach with faith.
And the one who invites the sons of the Church,
let him not doubt in his mind
that with the just and with the righteous
he will receive there a reward;
and he will be a companion to the saints,
and a wedding-guest at the nuptial banquet.

3.

And if they be little ones,
even with defects,
they will receive the reward of the righteous

in the great day of the resurrection.
Honour the priests
according to their rank,
and the deacons
according to their orders.
And to every son of the Church,
assign honour at all times:
they are ministers of God
and readers of the Book of Life.

4.

The Lord Himself, because you honoured them
in your dwelling for His sake,
and you stood as a servant before them[21]
and served them at your feast:
in the day of His coming He will make you recline,
He Christ, as He promised.[22]
And instead of the bread and wine which perished,
He will feed you with the Bread of Life.
And instead of the drink which does not remain,
He will refresh you together with the spiritual beings.

5.

O you, who received the disciples,
do not doubt in your mind,
that if you truly welcome them
you will abound a hundredfold,
as were increased the possessions
of righteous Job and of Abraham.
God who blessed
the house of just and righteous Abraham,
when He was received by him
under the oak in the desert,
He Himself will increase and multiply before you
His blessings, forever.
And you who welcomed His worshippers
in your tents because of your hope in Him,

in the tents of light you will rejoice
at the magnificence of His coming.

6.

And Christ for whose sake
you brought us into your dwellings,
He Himself will bring you into His bridal chamber
that you might be refreshed at His table.
May His grace sustain the elders
and make grow and preserve the young!
May grace strengthen the infirm,
and may they stand in Your strength, O Lord!
May grace give understanding to the readers,
lest they err in their readings!

7.

Let all of us give praise
to the Father who sent His Only-Begotten![23]
He came and redeemed us by His Cross
from the error of the idols.[24]
And He taught us how to answer saying:
One true God
who is known and proclaimed
in three divine persons.
To the chanter give profit
and to the listeners, benefit!
To all the company, delight,
and gladness to the master of the banquet!
To the Church and its children, exaltation,
forever and ever! Amen! Amen!

KEY TO ST EPHREM'S WRITINGS CITED IN NOTES

Nativity: Hymns on the Nativity
Julian: Hymns against Julian
Virginity: Hymns on Virginity

Ephrem the Syrian Hymns, trans. Kathleen McVey, (New York, Paulist Press, 1989).

Epiphany: Hymns for the Epiphany

The authentic ones, with excellent notes, may be found in *Efrem il Siro, Inni sulla Natività e sull' Epifania,* trans. I. De Francesco, (Milan, Paoline, 2003).

Unleavened Bread: Hymns on Unleavened Bread
Crucifixion: Hymns on the Crucifixion
Resurrection: Hymns on the Resurrection

Efrem il Siro, Inni Pasquali, trans. I. De Francesco, (Milan, Paoline, 2001).

Paradise: Hymns on Paradise

St Ephrem the Syrian, Hymns on Paradise, trans. S. P. Brock, (Crestwood, St Vladimir's Press, 1990).

Commentary on Genesis: Commentary on Exodus: Homily on Our Lord: Letter to Publius:

St Ephrem the Syrian, Selected Prose Works, trans. J. Amar and E. Mathews, *Fathers of the Church,* 91, (Washington, CUA, 1994).

Commentary on the Diatessaron:

St Ephrem's Commentary on Tatian's Diatessaron, trans Carmel McCarthy, *Journal of Semitic Studies,* Supplement 2, 1993.

A variety of Ephrem's writings may also be found in Gwynn:

A Select Library of Nicene and Post-Nicene Fathers of the Christian Church, ed. J. Gwynn, series two, vol. 13, (Oxford/New York, 1898; rept. Grand Rapids, 1983).

NOTES

Introduction

[1] *Interior Castle*, VI. 4. 15.

[2] See Abraham Isaac Kook, *In the Desert – a Vision (Midbar Shur)*, trans. Bezalel Naor, (Spring Valley, NY: Orot Inc., 2000): pp. 129-132.

[3] *Memra* III: 6; for this insight I am grateful to Ignazio De Francesco, as found in the Introduction to his Italian translation of the Table Blessings. See *La Gioia della Mensa*, trans. I. De Francesco (Magnano, Italy: Edizion I Quqajon, 2002).

[4] Commentary on the Diatessaron 19.4 as found in St Ephrem's Commentary on Tatian's Diatessaron, trans. Carmel McCarthy, Journal of Semitic Studies (Supplement 2. 1993).

[5] On the place of the created world in Ephrem's anthropology, see S. P. Brock, 'Humanity and the natural world in the Syriac tradition', *Sobornost/ECR* 12 (1990): pp. 131-142.

[6] From Hymn on Nisibis 50, as found in S. P. Brock, *The Harp of the Spirit: Eighteen Poems of St. Ephrem*, Studies Supplementary to *Sobornost*, 4, 2nd. ed. London, 1983.

[7] From Hymn on Faith 14, as found in Brock, *Harp of the Spirit*.

[8] Isaiah 61: 3; see S. P. Brock, 'The Robe of Glory: a biblical image in the Syriac tradition', *The Way* 39. 3 (1999): pp. 247-259.

[9] In Hymn on Faith 32, Ephrem attributes his own spiritual growth to praise:

> I stood in fear, having become aware of You;
> I grew because I magnified You.
> Whereas You do not thereby grow,
> The person who increases praise of Your Majesty
> Grows in You a great deal.

As found in S. P. Brock, *The Luminous Eye*, (Kalamazoo, MI: Cistercian Publications, 1992): p. 78.

[10] See P.Yousif, 'Le Repas fraternel ou l'agapé dans les mêmre sur la table attribués a Saint Ephrem', *Parole de l'Orient* 9 (1979/80): pp. 51-66.

[11] Yousif quotes briefly from the 12th century redaction of the *Expositio Officiorum Ecclesiae* of Ps. George of Arbela where a celebration is described which is similar to an *agape*. See Yousif, 'Repas fraternel', p. 65.

[12] See. T. Koonammakkal, 'Ephrem's Imagery of Chasm', *Symposium Syriacum* VII, ed. R. Lavenant (Rome, 1998): pp. 175-183. See also T. Koonammakkal, 'The Self-Revealing God and Man in Ephrem', *The Harp* 6. 3, (1993): pp. 233-248.

[13] Hymn on Faith 6. 17 as found in T. Koonammakkal, 'Ephrem on the Name of Jesus', *Studia Patristica.* 33 (Louvain 1997): pp 548-553. See also his 'Divine Names and Theological Language in Ephrem', *Studia Patristica* 25 (Louvain, 1993): pp. 318-323.

[14] I. Hausherr, *The Name of Jesus*, trans. Charles Cummings (Kalamazoo, MI: Cistercian Publications, 1978): pp. 42-52.

[15] For this schema see S. P. Brock, 'A Hymn of St Ephrem on the Eucharist', *The Harp* 1. 1 (1987): pp. 61-68. See also E. G. Mathews, 'St Ephrem, Madrase On Faith 81-85; Hymns on the Pearl, I-V', *St. Vladimir's Theological Quarterly* 38 (1994): pp. 45-72.

[16] This translation is my own but the complete hymn may be found in *Ephrem the Syrian: Hymns*, trans. Kathleen McVey (New York: Paulist Press, Classics of Western Spirituality, 1989). Included are all the Hymns on Virginity, especially of interest 28, 29 and 30, where Ephrem elaborates his symbolic theology. See also S. J. Beggiani, 'The Typological Approach of Syriac Sacramental Theology', *Theological Studies* 64 (2003): pp. 543-557.

[17] 'Creation gives birth to Christ in symbols as Mary did in the flesh' (Hymn on Virginity 6.8), as found in Brock, *Luminous Eye*, p. 56. These types and symbols are seen only by the eye of faith and here again it is praise which enhances the eye of faith, see Brock, *Luminous Eye*, p. 79.

[18] On the concept of divinization or *theosis* in Ephrem, see Brock, *Luminous Eye*, pp. 148-154.

[19] See Robert Murray, *Symbols of Church and Kingdom* (London; New York: Cambridge University Press, 1975): pp. 41-68. See also R. A. Darling, 'The "Church from the Nations" in the Exegesis of Ephrem', *Symposium Syriacum* IV, ed. H. J. W. Drijvers (Rome, 1987): pp. 111-121.

[20] Saber examines this singular aspect of Ephrem's theology. See Georges Saber, 'La Typologie Sacramentaire et Baptismal de St Éphrem', *Parole de l'Orient* 4 (1973): pp. 73-91, esp. pp. 83-84, 87.

[21] See Christine Shepardson, 'Anti-Jewish *Rhetoric* and Intra-Christian Conflict in the Sermons of Ephrem Syrus', *Studia Patristica* 35 (Louvain, 2001): pp. 502-507. See also Sidney H. Griffith, 'Ephraem, the Deacon of Edessa, and the Church of the Empire,' in *Diakonia: Studies in Honor of Robert T. Meyer*, ed. T. Halton and J. Williman (Washington, DC: 1986): pp. 22-52, esp. pp. 37-47 on the Arians.

[22] See P. J. Botha, 'Polarity: the Theology of anti-Judaism in Ephrem the Syrian's hymns on Easter', *Hervormde Teologiese Studies* 46, (1990): pp. 36-46.

[23] This is the term Bou Mansour uses in reference to both Ephrem's and Jacob's description of the relationship of 'the Nation and the Nations'. See

T. Bou Mansour, *La pensée symbolique de saint Éphrem le Syrien* (Kaslik/Lebanon: Bibliothèque de l'Université Saint-Esprit, 16, 1988): pp. 322-328; 342-343. See also his *La théologie de Jacques de Saroug*, 2 vols. (Kaslik/Lebanon: Bibliothèque de l'Université Saint-Esprit, 36 1993; 40, 2000). See vol. 1, pp. 171-181; vol. 2, pp. 387-392.

[24] About this mystery, Golitzin reminds concerning the Syriac tradition that it is: '… a fundamental biblical, and yes Jewish-based understanding of the redemption and salvation offered by Jesus Messiah … Jacob and his fellow Syrians, from Aphrahat and Ephrem to Isaac of Nineveh—and even Dionysius the Areopagite … help to demonstrate that our Christian roots are planted firmly in the land of Israel.'

See Alexander Golitzin, 'The Image and Glory of God in Jacob of Jacob of Serug's Homily, "On that Chariot that Ezekiel the Prophet Saw"', *St Vladimir's Theological Quarterly* 47: 3-4, (2003): pp. 323-364, esp. pp 360-364.

[25] Homily 75 as found in P.Bedjan, ed., *Homiliae Selectae Mar-Jacobi Sarugensis I-V*, (Paris/Leipzig, 1905-10), vol. III (1907): pp. 208-223. The translation cited here is from 'A Homily on Our Lord and Jacob, on the Church and Rachel, and on Leah and the Synagogue', *The True Vine* 4: 4 (1993): pp. 50-64, see verses 223-238. A similar approach appears in Aphrahat: 'David married two kings' daughters and Jesus also married two kings' daughters—the assembly of the People and the assembly of the Peoples', (Demonstration 21. 13), as found in Brock, *Luminous Eye*, p. 117.

Memra I

[1] Essence (*'îṯûṯâ*), according to de Halleux, the term in Ephrem's writings never has the philosophical sense of *ousia* but always denotes the living God of the burning bush (Exod. 3: 2). See André de Halleux, 'Saint Éphrem le Syrien', *Revue Théologique de Louvain* 14 (1983): p. 347. On the theological value of various Syriac terms used by Ephrem including *'îṯûṯâ, 'iṯyâ, kyânâ*, and *qnômâ* see J. F. Bethune Baker, *Nestorius and his Teaching*, (New York, Kraus Reprint, 1969): pp. 212-232. See also U. Possekel, *Evidence of Greek Philosophical Concepts in the Writings of Ephrem the Syrian, Corpus Scriptorum Christianorum Orientalium*, p. 580, subs. 102 (Louvain 1999): pp. 55-74.

[2] Cf. John 4: 14.

[3] Word/silence: for Ephrem, what defines humans is that they speak. See for example *Paradise* 8. 8. El-Khoury examines this aspect of the word in Ephrem. See N. el-Khoury, 'Gen. 1. 26 dans l'interprétation de Saint Éphrem ou la relation de l'homme à Dieu', *Symposium Syriacum* II, *Orientalia Christiana Analecta* 205 (Rome 1978): pp. 199-205. On the importance of 'word' in Jacob of Serug, see Bou Mansour, *Jacques de Saroug*, vol. 2, pp. 436-442. But the silence or mutism of the animals seen here is not

to be confused with silence as described by many Syriac writers. For example, John the Solitary says 'God is silence'. See S. P. Brock, 'John the Solitary, on Prayer', *Journal of Theological Studies* 30 (1979): pp. 84-101.

[4] Cf. James 2: 3-4.

[5] Table of the Kingdom, see *Paradise* 2. 5; 7. 24; 11. 15; Ephrem's *Letter to Publius* 21. On the eschatological sense of kingdom (*malkûtâ*) and the particular way early Syriac writers understood it, see Murray, *Symbols*, pp. 239-246. See also various aspects of *malkûtâ* in Jacob of Serug's writings; see Bou Mansour, *Jacques de Saroug*, vol. 2, pp. 222-252.

[6]. Cf. Luke 16: 19-31.

[7]. Matt. 25: 35.

[8]. Cf. Gen. 18: 1-15.

[9]. Cf. Jer. 35.

[10]. Cf. Num. 6: 1-4.

[11]. Cf. I Tim. 5: 23.

[12]. Gen. 9: 21; 19: 33-35.

[13]. Watchers (*'îrê*): the Syriac tradition frequently designates angels as watchers (Daniel 4: 13, 17). Sometimes the term means angel, other times one of the Cherubim and Seraphim. Watchers figure prominently in the Pseudepigrapha and in later Jewish mystical literature, such as 3 Enoch, a Merkabah text, where they are actually a separate order: 'Above all these are four great princes called Watchers ... their abode is opposite the throne of glory ... they receive glory from the glory of the Almighty and are praised with the praise.' 3 Enoch 28: 1-3. See also P. J. Botha, 'Fire Mingled with Spirit: St Ephrem's Views on Angels and the Angelic Life of Christians', *The Harp* 8-9 (1995): pp. 95-104. Christ is also called a Watcher or 'Wakeful One' (*Nativity* 21. 4) who has come to make us watchers. See Brock, *Luminous Eye*, pp. 140-141.

Memra II

[1] Sustainer of the universe/of all: *za'en kul*. As a divine title the term appears in other of Ephrem's hymns: *Paradise* 9. 8; *Crucifixion* 3. 17; *Nativity* 11: 8; *Resurrection* 1: 17. See also Acts of Thomas 19. The term has great importance in the fourth-century Book of Steps: 'He who provides everything (*za'en kul*) can provide for all in need ... God in fact wanted these things to be this way; wanted all humanity to praise him without having to work' (3. 15). 'So it was for Adam while he lived according to the will of God and God fed (*za'en*) him as it was appropriate to the wealth of his kindness with heavenly bread' (21. 7). God still guides every creature to understand that He created and sustains (*za'en*) them' (9.16), 'and by the

Spirit leads them to proclaim God as "Creator and Sustainer of everything"' (5. 15). See also 10. 6; 20. 13; 22. 13; 25. 3. See Robert A. Kitchen and Martien F. G. Parmentier, *The Book of Steps* (Kalamazoo, MI: Cistercian Publications, 2004).

[2] Cf. Matt. 10: 4.

[3] Proferred: *yšṭ*, give/extend.

Memra III

[1] The contrast between visible/invisible and hidden/revealed is found throughout Ephrem's writings. One might say that it is fundamental to his anthropology. According to Brock, Ephrem uses hidden/revealed in two different ways: the 'human experience of God's hiddeness (*kasyûṭâ*) is only possible through God's various instances of self-revelation'; then there is 'not the human experience of God, but God's actual Being (*'îṭûṭâ*), which objectively exists, but which can only be experienced in a hidden and subjective way'. For this important distinction, see *Luminous Eye*, pp. 27-29. For other examples, see *Paradise*: 1. 1, 2; 7. 12; 10. 1; 11. 5, 12. 16; *Homily on Our Lord*, Section I. See also Koonammakkal, 'Self-Revealing God'. See G. Noujaim, 'Anthropologie et économie de salut chez saint Éphrem autour des actions *Ghalyaṭa, Kasyaṭa, et Kasya, Parole de l'Orient* 9 (1979/80): pp.313-315.

[2] Cf. John 6: 14.

[3] Cf. Luke 23: 31; Graffin sees in this a possible allusion to the Cross. See Graffin, 'Mimre', p. 94.

[4] Cf. John 2: 10. For the relation of Cana to the Eucharist, according to Ephrem, see his beautiful Hymn on Faith 14, in Brock, *Harp of the Spirit.*

[5] Vine-dresser/ploughman (*palâhâ*): title of Christ. See *Nativity* 3. 14-15; *Paradise* 14. 13. See also Murray, *Symbols*, pp. 195-197.

[6] See Introduction for comments on Adam's sin and this singular interpretation of it.

[7] Cf. Gen. 3: 6.

[8] Continuing the reflection on Adam's sin, Ephrem suggests that it is in the Cenacle that Christ restores all by His giving thanks.

[9] Broke (bread) *qsâ*: the word used for the Eucharistic offering as well as for the multplication of the loves, Matt.14: 19, 26: 26, Luke 22: 19, I Cor: 11: 24. The Eucharistic loaf itself is called *qsâṭâ*. In the *Commentary on the Diatessaron* 19. 4, the full meaning emerges of Christ's self-immolation, breaking Himself: 'From the moment when *he broke* his body for his disciples and *gave it* to his apostles, three days are numbered during which

he was counted among the dead, like Adam.' And in Hymn on Faith 48, conserved in Armenian, Ephrem says:

> It was the very same Christ in the Upper Room
>   who gave and was distributed to all.
> Even though the People slew Him,
>   He had previously slain Himself with His own hand.
> It was one slain by His own hands
>   that the crazed ones crucified on Golgotha,
> had He not slain Himself in symbol,
>   they would not have slain Him in actual fact.

(Armenian hymns 48, lines 41-48)

Translation found in Brock, *Luminous Eye*, p. 102. See also Francois Graffin, 'L'Eucharistie chez saint Éphrem', *Parole de_l'Orient* 4 (1973): 95. For other examples of *qsâ* in relation to Christ's sacrifice, see *Unleavened Bread* 2: 7, 12: 5, 14: 23, 19: 1-2; *Crucifixion* 3: 5, 9; *Resurrection* 3: 16.

Memra IV

[1] Cf. Dan. 1: 12.

[2] Cf. I Kings 19: 1-8.

[3] Ezek. 1:3; 4: 9.

[4] II Kings 6: 25.

[5] I Kings 17: 6.

[6] II Kings 4: 38-41

[7] Cf. Matt. 14:11.

[8] Cf. I Sam. 2: 12-14.

[9] People ('*ammâ*), the Jewish Nation, see Murray, *Symbols*, pp. 41-68. See also Dominique Cerbelaud, 'L'Antijudaïsme dans les Hymnes de Pascha d'Éphrem le Syrien', *Parole de l'Orient* 20 (1995): pp. 201-207. Cerbelaud gives a balanced approach to anti-Jewish themes in Ephrem.

[10] Cf. Num. 11: 20.

[11] Cf Exod. 32: 6.

[12] Cf. Exod.32: 19, Peshitta, where the presence of symbols is noted.

Memra V

[1] For a discussion of Ephrem's symbolic understanding of the Trinity through the sun and its light and its heat, see Bou Mansour, *Pensée Symbolique*, pp. 201-217. In three hymns this theme is developed at length:

Faith 40 in S. P. Brock, *A Garland of Hymns from the Early Church* (Maclean, Virginia, 1989); *Faith* 73 in Brock, *Harp of the Spirit* ; *Faith* 74 in Sidney H. Griffith, 'St Ephrem the Syrian, a Spiritual Teacher for Today', *The Harp* 16 (2002): pp. 185-189.

[2] Cf. I Sam. 20: 24.

[3] Eat, *'ekal*; the Syriac word includes a sense of accusation or slander such as is referred to in this stanza.

[4] . Cf. Gen. 37: 25.

[5] Cf. Gen. 43: 31-34.

[6] 'Wine ... in our veins', is used by Ephrem to describe the Eucharist, cf. *Virginity* 37. 2:

> Christ's Body has newly been mingled with our bodies,
> His Blood too has been poured out into our veins,
> His voice is in our ears,
> His brightness in our eyes.
> In His compassion the whole of Him has been mingled
> in with the whole of us.

As found in Brock, *Luminous Eye*, pp. 105-106.

Memra VI

[7] People, *'ammâ*, Jewish Nation.

[8] Cf. Exod. 16.

[9] Cf. Exod 17: 1-7. Early rabbinic tradition saw this Rock as a messianic symbol. One aspect of this tradition may be found in Louis Ginzberg, *Legends of the Bible* (Philadelphia, PA: Jewish Publication Society of America, 1956): pp. 369-37. On 'Christ the Rock', and other of its meanings, see Murray, *Symbols*, pp. 205-238.

[10] Merciful One: *Paradise* 7. 9; *Homily on Our Lord* 48. 2.

[11] At the Incarnation, God 'put on a body' (Nativity 9. 2). And Ephrem applies the image of the body as the garment of Christ to the Eucharist, thereby adding a Eucharistic dimension to all bread. 'You have two garments, Our Lord: the garment, both the body and the bread, the life-giving bread' (*Faith* 19. 2). See T. Koonammakkal, 'Ephrem's Polemics on the Human Body', *Studia Patristica* 35 (Louvain, 2001): pp. 428-432. See also Sidney H. Griffith, '"Spirit in the Bread; Fire in the Wine": the Eucharist as "Living Medecine" in the Thought of Ephrem the Syrian', *Modern Theology* 15.2 (1999): pp. 225-246.

[12] In Syriac, *rûhâ* means both wind and spirit/Spirit. See *Paradise* 9. 7-17, where the power of wind/air to sustain all life is described.

Memra VII

[1] Num. 13: 23-25. According to Robert Murray the cluster (*sgôlâ*) of grapes brought back from Canaan, seen also in *Nativity* 1. 30, is for Ephrem a type of Christ on the Cross. And Murray sees all of *Memra* VII to be Ephrem's reflection on the ingratitude of Israel despite the bringing back of the cluster. See Murray, *Symbols*, pp. 119. Cluster and grape imagery, as symbols of Christ and the Eucharist, occur throughout Ephrem's writings: *Nativity* 3. 15; 4. 27; 8. 8; 24. 17; *Virginity* 11. 11; 31. 13; *Faith* 12. 8; *Paradise* 6. 8; *Crucifixion* 3. 9; *Commentary on the Diatessaron* 1. 27. See also Aphrahat, 'Demonstration' 23.

[2] Exod. 32: 4; Deut. 9: 16; Acts 7: 41.

[3] Grape, *'enbâ*, found throughout this *Memra* for grape, rather than *tûtîtâ* commonly used by Ephrem in reference to Christ.

[4] All occurences of people (*'ammâ*) in this *Memra* refer to the Jewish Nation, see Note 9, *Memra* IV.

[5] Bitter/sweet, one of the many paradoxes Ephrem uses in his symbolic approach. For other examples of this paradox, see: *Paradise* 7. 14; 9. 2; 11. 10; 12. 3; 15. 13. See also *Nativity* 1. 89; 13. 4; 14. 3; 18. 26; 24. 7; 28. 8. On Ephrem's use of paradox, see Brock, *Luminous Eye*, pp. 23-25.

[6] Ps 80: 8; 'You are a sprig of that vine from Egypt which the wild boar of the forest had eaten when it sprouted and went out from the shoot which brought forth the blessed Cluster and the cup of the Medicine of Life.' (*Faith* 12. 8); *Crucifixion* 5. 9; *Julian*, On the Church 9; *Commentary on Genesis* 42. 5. 4; Aphrahat, Demonstration 19. 5.

[7] Here Ephrem may be saying that ingratitude lies within all hearts, whether gentile or Jew, and that human freedom and free will (*hêrutâ*), so important to Ephrem's theology, is what matters. In the *Letter to Publius*, Ephrem's vision of the last judgment, the 'tribes' of Israel and the nations stand together at the time of reckoning. See *Letter to Publius*, 5. On *hêrutâ*: see Brock, *Luminous Eye*, pp. 34-36; A. de Halleux, 'Mar Éphrem Théologien', *Parole de l'Orient* 4 (1973): pp. 50-53. See also T. Bou Mansour, 'La liberté chez S. Éphrem le Syrien', *Parole de l'Orient* 11 (1983): pp. 89-156.

Memra VIII

[1] Num. 21: 6.

[2] Num. 26: 10.

[3] Num. 16: 32.

[4] Cf. Num. 11: 33.

[5] Cf. Num. 11: 20.

[6] Type (*tûpsâ*): types and symbols are everywhere since God created the world. 'Creation gives birth to Christ in symbols, as Mary did in the flesh' (*Virginity* 6 .8). But they can only be seen by the eye of faith. And learning to see this way, one develops an ecological way of looking at the world. See Introduction, note 17.

[7] Luke 16.

[8] Scripture and creation are full of symbols which can never be grasped by scrutiny. A rational, purely intellectual approach, will never open up what is not only described but contained within the symbol. Ephrem, and other Fathers of the Syriac tradition, rejected discursive reasoning and those inquirers (*bâsôyê*) like Arius who tried to scrutinize the nature of God rather than discerning the mystery, in wonder. But Ephrem's approach, guided by faith, was never anti-intellectual. See '*Faith*' 8. 9; 9. 16; '*Nativity*' 3. 5; 25. 1; 25. 14; '*Epiphany*' 10. 19. See Brock, *Luminous Eye*, pp. 26-27. See also Koonammakkal, 'Imagery of Chasm', pp. 175-183. On Ephrem and the Arians see, Griffith, 'Deacon of Edessa', pp. 37-47. Jacob of Serug also strongly rejected scrutiny, see Bou Monsour, *Jacques de Saroug*, vol. 2, pp. 448-461.

Memra X

[1] Ephrem has left us a grid for the understanding of all reality, including 'beings above and those below'. Types and symbols operate for Ephrem horizontally between Old and New Testaments and vertically between God and creatures. In the vertical dimension, angels are above and often called by Ephrem as 'heavenly' or 'beings above' in contrast with humans who are 'earthly' or 'those below'. Angels are superior to humans by their nature, yet by grace only persons are called 'sons of the Most High' (Ps. 82.6), according to Ephrem. On this relation between angels and humans, see Botha, 'Fire Mingled'. For the grid, see R. Murray, 'Symbolism in St.Ephrem's Theology', *Parole de l'Orient* 6-7 (1975-76): 3-9.

[2] Cf. Gen. 4: 4.

[3] Cf. Job 42: 10.

[4] Cf. Matt. 14: 20.

[5] Cf. I Kings 17: 12

[6] Cf. I Kings 17: 14-16.

[7] Cf. Deut. 33.

[8] In rabbinical exegesis an early Midrash quotes Moses as saying: 'May Reuben come to life again in the future life for his good deed in saving

Joseph' (Gen 37: 22) 'and may he not remain forever dead on account of his sin with Bilhah' (Gen 35: 22). Another Midrash adds 'that Reuben never asked his father's pardon, and therefore his sin, notwithstanding his life-long repentance, was not forgiven until Moses prayed for him'. See L. Ginzberg, *Legends of the Jews* (Baltimore: Johns Hopkins Univ. Press, 1998): vol. 3, p. 485; vol. 6, pp. 154-155. The prayer of Moses is also seen by some to be a sign of the future resurrection: *'Let Reuben live and not die*: But was he not already dead? What does Scripture mean by *and not die*? In the world to come.' (Sifre Deuteronomy 347). Aphrahat also notes the pardon of Reuben in the light of the future resurrection, see Demonstration 8. 8.

[9] Bridal chamber, *gnônâ*, is often used by Ephrem to describe the kingdom, either eschatological or as realized on earth. In the *Commentary on the Diatessaron* he says:

> During the entire period that Our Lord
> was in the midst of the world, he compared
> it to a bridal chamber, and himself to the
> bridegroom. (5. 22a)

See also *Paradise* 1. 6; 7. 15. 24; 13. 3. 10; *Letter to Publius* 12. The theme appears in other early Syriac literature: Odes of Solomon 11; Acts of Thomas 9-15; 124; Aphrahat 6. 1 , 6; Book of Steps 19. 36; 20. 6, 14. For various aspects in Ephrem, including the bridal chamber of the heart, see Brock, *Luminous Eye*, pp. 115-130.

[10] John 2: 1-11; see Hymn on Faith 14, in Brock, *Harp of the Spirit*.

[11] This sentence is noted by Graffin as a gloss.

[12] Cf. Matt.14: 18.

[13] Cf. Luke 19: 8.

[14] Cf. Mark 14: 15, but here probably upper room refers to the house of Zacchaeus, as for example in Acts 9: 37-39; 20: 8, where it is also used in describing local houses.

[15] To clothe a body, here refers to the Incarnation. Clothing imagery may be found throughout Scripture in reference to God and humanity. The early Syriac tradition describes all of salvation history using clothing imagery. See S. P. Brock, 'Clothing Metaphors as a Means of Theological Expression', *Typus, Symbol, Allegorie bei den ostlichen Vatern und ihren Parallelen im mittelalter*. ed. M. Schmidt (Eichstatter Beitrage 4, Eichstatt: 1982): pp. 11-40. See also Brock, 'Robe of Glory', pp. 247-259.

[16] Cf. Luke 19: 10.

[18] Matt 10: 41.

[19] Cf. Gen.18: 1-15.

[20] Cf. Matt 13: 8.

[21] Cf. Gen. 18: 8.

[22] Cf. Luke 12: 37.

[23] Only-Begotten, *Îhîd̲âyâ*, a title of Christ, but the term in the early Syriac tradition was applied to all baptized Christians, especially to the ascetics. See T. K. Koonammakkal, 'Ephrem's Ideas on Singleness', *Hugoye* 2. 1 (1999). See also Sidney Griffith, '"Singles in God's Service": thoughts on the Ihidaya from the works of Aphrahat and Ephraem the Syrian', *The Harp* 4 (1991): pp. 145-159.

[24] Ephrem describes the fallen human condition as a 'state of sickness' (*krîhuṭâ*) as does St Paul (e.g. Rom 5: 6; 6: 19; 8: 3, 26). Because of this state, error can enter in and become a disease. The 'error of idols' is linked to paganism which Ephrem considers to be a disease of the soul:

> Because he poured out his grace among them, idolatry fled before him, and their paganism took off into the Gentiles. And it was as if they, when the time was fulfilled, were healed of the illness of error. Their idolatry betook itself far from the rays of the Life-Giver, and through the constraint of his miracles the people's paganism deserted them. (*Commentary on the Diatessaron* 11. 6)

God, the 'ultimate Healer', wills to heal humanity. Ephrem calls healing a 'second creation'. According to Shemunkasho in his interpretation of Ephrem: 'As God created the world, Jesus fulfilled it by his healing.' See Aho Shemunkasho, *Healing in the Theology of St Ephrem* (Piscataway, NJ: Gorgias Press, 2002): pp. 294-303; 325-328; 407-413. See also A. Shemunkasho, 'Salvation History as a Process of Healing in the Theology of Mor Ephrem', *The Harp* 11-12 (1998/99): pp. 175-185.